Women!

A Poetic Tribute

Mahdy Y. Khaiyat

WOMEN! A Poetic Tribute

Cover photograph by Ana Ruth Flores.

Published by M. K. Publishing
P. O. Box 1265, Goleta, CA 93116

(805) 968-0040
mahdy10@cox.net

ISBN-10: 0985918845
ISBN-13: 978-0-9859188-4-2

FOREWORD

When I was four years old, I developed the habit of plucking a rose from the garden, giving it to my mother, and basking in her smile.

Today, when a woman discloses her smile to me, a feeling of warmth waltzes through me. A women's smile has such a magical effect!

In this book, there are poems that speak of women's beauty, charm, and personal strengths. In others, women protest their treatment quietly and vociferously.

This book contains those poems which are about women: their movements, their looks, and their mystery.

TABLE OF CONTENTS

THE BIRTH OF VENUS

A PAINTING BY SANDRO BOTTICELLI, 1440-1510

Emerging from the womb's secret passages,
She stands on the incandescent vessel,
Scintillating cryptic smiles.

Jasmine blossoms, wings of temptation,
Swirl about her glowing skin,
Diffusing incense, pollinating the imagination.

Men rejoice: Such mesmerizing beauty!

LES DEMOISELLES D'AVIGNON, 1907

A PAINTING BY PICASSO

Women!

Their curves, which feed fantasies and inspire melodies,
Whose sinuous moves topple castles and empires are
Reduced to crude lines, giving distortion and ugliness
Painterly prominence.

The virtuoso's intent may have been to topple women
From their pedestals and reduce them to a more human
Level, where the female sexual power is acknowledged,
But not glorified.

DESERT AND RIVER

A man is a desert.
A woman is a river;
Her ancient flow
Makes the desert
    Bloom.

IT MUST BE A WOMAN

The heels tap softly and
Rhythmically.

The aroma slowly
Diffuses,
Mingling with the rising scent
Of roses and hyacinths.

The steps grow louder and louder.

The anticipation is keen.
Moments dissolve quickly.

As I glimpse her face.
The red roses bow.

MY ROSE

When she smells like a rose,
When she dances like a rose,
When she sashays like a rose,
When she responds to her
Admirers like a rose; she is a rose,

    She is my Rose.

JACARANDA

Among the trees
Queuing the street
The jacaranda stands out
Like a beauty queen.
She tosses her
Lavender progeny
Into the swirling air;
They dance
Like tipsy ballerinas
Before touching the sidewalk
And weaving a floral rug.

THE ROSE AND THE DAISY

The red rose boasts,
"Do you see me flutter?
Do you smell my fragrance?"

"I know you're beautiful.
But I don't want to be
Like you," Replies the daisy.

A gentleman happens by, plucks
The rose and offers it to his lady.

The daisy sighs.

ONE NEVER KNOWS

Lavender-bloused,
She moved like a lily
Shimmering
In the pale evening Sun.

The soft wind teased
Her dark blond hair
Into a jumble, and
Her immaculately-
Polished fingernails,
Trying to repair
The damage,
Incarnadined the air.

As she passed by me,
She threw the displaced
Air into my face,

And I thought lilies
Had a pleasant fragrance!

THE DANCING MAIDENS OF VIENNA

Like the agile lemurs of Madagascar,
The dancing maidens leap gracefully
Into the air and fall back on the firm
Terrain. Attired in flowing diaphanous
Robes, of soft blue and peach, their
Bodies fold and unfold rhythmically
As if their flesh and bones were mingled
In a flexible mass of clay. As they float
In waltzing clouds over the Blue Danube,
Their swirling motions mime the melodic
Passions of Johann Strauss. They dance
And dance and dance till their delicate
                    Forms fade into the mist.

MANDOLIN

She is my latest.
Look at her
Reclining on the ottoman
Like an indescribably beautiful woman.
Her bejeweled and slightly bent neck
Appears to be ready for stroking.
Sleek and stringy, her midriff
Is sensitive to the touch.
Her womb is
A cornucopia of melodies.
Ah, strum her right
And she will deliver a beautiful baby!

A FACE IN THE MIRROR

She sits in a bench,
Pulls out a mirror.
Ah, a perfect face,
A Marilyn Monroe clone.
The eye of my red-blooded
Fantasy swells.

Full face in the mirror,
Her eyes seem to stare,
Scanning a hidden terrain.
A slight grin brightens
Her lips, perhaps remembering
Sashaying to an evening
Rendezvous with an angel of love,
Or expecting a promise to carry her off
To her field of dreams.

As I amble away,
Her mirrored face
Dances within me.

SYMPHONY

Arise, my Love, arise!

The songstress has strummed
The harp of dawn, and the
Painter has brushed the
Sky red and gold.

Place your dreams under the
Pillow till the crickets
Call us to bed.

Wash your face with the
Morning scent and glow
For its petals will soon
Wilt and go.

Let's sip our nectar under
The lucent sky and listen
To the swallows while we
May, for we will soon be
Squirreled away in the
File of Fate.

Arise, my Love, arise!

TO THE MOON

The veins on
Your face, au naturel,
Painted on papyrus,
Or etched in stone,
Are hieroglyphics
Read with glee.

Strolling or
Standing still,
You rain
Nuggets or doubloons.

The wounded and
The smitten
Make the pilgrimage
To your feet.

The high and
The low
Moan
Whenever you're gone
        Or obscured.

THE PERSIAN RUG

On the pink bed,
The irises and daffodils
Rising
From lace of
Verdant vines;
On the borders,
Flaming red squares
Guard
All entrances to the
Palace of Rosebuds
Where
You and I
Are marooned.

GHAZAL*

Flowers are associated with romance and love.
A woman likes to get flowers when she's in love.

A bruised rose is not nearly as desirable.
A smooth rose represents an unblemished love.

Imperfect rose petals may signify bruised feelings,
Which should not happen if one wishes to keep her love.

Someone once placed a bouquet of flowers next to
My door; was it out of pity or out of love?

Mahdy says: Whatever the motive was, receiving
Flowers from a woman involves a romance and love.

*A form of Persian verse or a piece of Arabic music with
a frequent refrain

FLOWER

The flower in the
Exquisitely-arranged bouquet
Is eager to tell the one
Left in the garden
How fortunate she is!

OH, HYACINTH

You boast of your
Innocence.

Your smile
And your words
Diverge.

Your sophisticated
Aroma
Spreads shivers,
Inflames the imagination.

Your eyes
Guard
The secret
Of your intent.

LILY OF THE NILE

Tall and lissome,
She defies the
Customary measure
Of grace as she dances
In the afternoon breeze.

Pre-dawn witnesses
An invading storm
Twist her neck;
She bleeds to martyrdom.

BROCADE

Clusters of stars scintillate
    In the low blue sky.
The Moon lases her smile
    At the water.
On the edge of the bank,
    The daffodils,
    The hyacinths,
    And the red roses
Bend their necks and see their reflections
As a sluggish wave
Waltzes toward the shallows—
    Unfolding a brocade.

CRYSTAL

Her hair!
Her auburn hair!

Dropping from
Top to ankle
Like
A bead curtain
Swinging
Splitting
revealing

In bed
It rests on either side
Of the incarnadine dunes.

A FRIEND IN A HIGH PLACE

At dusk
She follows me
Wherever I go.

She sometimes stumbles into tall trees,
Disappears behind large buildings,
Bumps into power lines
Which break her face to pieces,
Somehow she manages to put it back together.

When I reach home
I take a last look at her round golden face
And feel exhilarated to have
A beautiful friend is such a high place.

EVENING

The young balmy evening
Throws her long black hair
Over my face and shoulders.
Her soft, glistening eyes
Demolish my last defenses.
Cooing sounds send
The unmistakable message
Of chastity's flight
Into the estrum of night.

ANDALUSIAN

Sloe-eyed, kohl-lined,
Svelt-waisted, doe-skinned,
Sashaying
Through my blooming mind,
Spreading jasmine,
Sprinkling smiles in
The cortege of my despair.

EURASIAN

High cheekbones,
The peaks of two worlds,
Pride of synthesis.

Her red-tinged hair
Shines in the sun.
As she hops on virgin grass,
Her smile streams to adoring stares.

She is in the eye,
Yet distant.
I shatter
And before I gather the pieces,
She scurries away
And I cry.

THE AIR

Between us is what keeps us from being closer.

THE JOGGER ON LOS CARNEROS ROAD

The Sun shines
On her ribboned ponytail
Alternating
Bright and pale gold.

She turns around;
Her fair, untanned face
Gleams
As it moves ahead of
The dancing stalks of wheat.

SOSTENUTO

Long before the Moon
Nudges the Sun
Into his majestic appearance,
The songbirds receive cues
From the maestro
To begin their sostenuto.
In this crisp autumn night,
You and I
Engage in our own sostenuto
On the bed of love.

HEMLOCK OF YOUR SWEET TALK

You make me
Swallow the bitterweed
Of your rejection
While the honey
Of your love streams
Into the palates
Of other lovers,
And when I complain,
You force me to sip
The hemlock
Of your sweet talk.

JUST AS

There is no such thing
As everlasting love,
There is no such thing
As fire without ash.

THE LOVEBIRD

On its wings,
I fly into
Unknown dimensions.

Under its feathers,
I seek safety.

From its beak,
I receive nourishment.

Against its talons,
I cling.

From its talons,
I fall and sink.

THE SCORPIONS OF ILLUSION

I shall not be mesmerized
By her Christy Brinkley beauty.
I shall not be tantalized
By her Madison-Avenue struts.
I shall not be swayed
By her Rome-designed skirts.
I shall not surrender my dignity
To her Ipanema-styled bikinis.
I shall not be entranced
By her Paris-blended fragrance.

No!
I shall not be stung.
I shall not be stung.

I shall scorn the scorpions
Of illusion—

As long as I am dead!

TONIGHT

The harp and the cello
Cascade;
The drizzle pearls
Our skin.

Your lips, rosebuds,
Unfurl to crimson-red.

The mystery of the night
Burrows in the hollows
Of your cheeks.

MIDNIGHT

A neighbor's bed
Upstairs
Dances
To familiar rhythms.

Then silence.

The bathroom faucet
Flows.

Silence.

THE VIOLINIST

The violin,

The wounded animal

Under her thumb,

Ferrets out melodies

From the jungle

Of her unconscious.

PEAR

Pear!
> You're sturdy and volatile.
> You pay no attention to me.

Pear!
> You're full and supple.
> You laugh at my persistence.

Pear!
> You've changed to an apple
> And I to a bent twig.

THE ROMANTIC RENDEZVOUS

Finally,
Here we are
Together—alone.

Romantic music,
A crackling fireplace,
A lacy cloth draping
The dining table,
Crystal glasses,
Polished silverware,
Gourmet cuisine,
A bouquet of roses,
Flickering candlelight.

"Turn on the lights;
I want to see my food—
And that music makes
Me nervous!"
    She blurts.

THE LURE

We spend our lives
Going,
Going somewhere.

We never stop;
We keep going,
Going somewhere.
No one knows where,
Here or there.
We keep going,
Going somewhere.

There must be
Something ahead.
We keep going,
Going somewhere.
There must be
Something ahead.

TEA, VERSES, AND YOU

A cup of tea, steaming,
Lines of verses rushing
Through my fingertips,
And you,
You sitting pretty
On the ancient couch
Stealing glimpses
Of a world yet to be!

THE LURE OF SPONTANEITY

The cure it provides for
The wakened instincts;
The fruits of serendipity
It yields
In the whorls of exploration;
The cheeks of contentment
Flushing
In the air's embrace.

MIXED SIGNALS

Your eyes say
You are as impenetrable
As the depths of the ocean.

Your body says
You are as shallow as
       A bathtub.
         Why then do I fear drowning?

COBALT BLUE

The cobalt blue sky
Strikes at my center.

The cobalt blue sea
Splashes out
Of a Picasso painting
        And drowns me!

The Samurai warrior jumps
Out of a cobalt blue tapestry
And brandishes his sword.

The cobalt blue arrows
Of your eyes
Pierces my chest

        And paint it red!

THE COLOR RED

The earth's blood
Seeps through
The tree's veins
Making cherries

Which paint
Your lips and tongue
Glossy ruby and carmine—

Leaving my lips
And tongue
     In flames!

COED

She discourses on Spinoza and Nietzsche
With the facility and aplomb
Of a seasoned professor.
She discusses quantum physics
Like an accomplished scientist.
She can recite Shakespearean sonnets
Or write her own epic poems.

When she strolls on the beach
Strangers whistle and sigh.

SUCCESSFUL WOMEN

The question is not
Whether men are afraid
Of successful women.
Rather, men are fearful
That women would descend
To the level
Of successful men.

DISTAFF

So she slips
Into something
More comfortable:
A pair of tight jeans,
A high-neck sweatshirt—

And a cryptic smile.

MELODIES

Wearing a low-cut dress
And bustling on high heels,
Her well-shaped melodies
Rise and fall,
Pleading the Sun for a tan,
Forgiving the frigid air
For the encroachment.

Admirers linger;
Their eyes
Shuttle between pleasure and despair.

A smile dances on her lips.

GIMLET-EYED BEAUTY

Coming from the opposite street,
She shoots furtive glances at me.
As our paths converge,
This gimlet-eyed beauty
Discloses her smile
And my energy swells.

YOU EXPECT ME TO . . .

You dress
Like a bird of paradise
And expect me
           To be color-blind.

You spread your fragrance
           Like a musk duck
And expect me
To be immune to scent.

You croon
Like a robin
And expect me
To be deaf as a mountain.

You protrude
Your feminine charms
And expect me
To behave like a rutless tiger.

You tuck away
Your inhibitions
And expect me
To react like a mummified Egyptian.

DAWN

The tears pearling your cheeks
Tell a thousand stories; the
Theatre is empty. You remain
Cloistered in silence.

Minutes trudge like defeated
Armies; soon your eyes can see
The tonsured landscape—
Nothing to fill it, nothing.

Day merges into night; night
Into dawn. Outside the window
You watch the mist spiral down;
Leaves display their beads.

A butterfly smile lands on your
Lips; rivers of thought are
Rushing out.

COME TO ME

Come to me
With no awareness of time.
Bring no roses
Or carnations—
Only daisies
Or chrysanthemums.

Come to me
With no awareness of time.
Bring no regrets
Or worries—
Only the freedom of egrets
And the tunes of canaries.

Come to me
With no awareness of time.
Let mingle the honey of our saliva;
Let it seal our interlocked forms
Like the meandering lava does
The crevices and curves of Java.

WATER LILY

So long, Lily.
So long, my Lily.

As you float
And blossom,
I wither and
Sink;
The muddy water
Below
Keeps pulling me
Away from
Your canopy.

As I go,
I know you will
Kiss the wind.
I know you will.

Someday
We may understand,
Someday.

Take care, Lily.
Take care.
Take care.

YOUR ABSENCE

In the taciturnity
Of night,
I hold your absence;
I hold your absence
Ever so tight—

Before the morning
Quivers and bares
My flow,
My secret flow.

LONELY

When I am lonely
I like to see you,
But I won't.
I would like to,
But I can't.
I want to,
But I won't.

VICTORIA'S SECRET

The models strut and sashay
Without end.
Their eyes gesture,
Induce.

Their nimble limbs move ahead
Of their flamboyant bodies;
They seduce.

We try to catch
      What they toss.
We touch them with our
Eyes and senses.

They enter our
Collective unconscious
Through the subliminal
And the egregious;
 They take root.

EXCHANGE

She gives me a quick glance.
I give her a faint smile.
My eyes follow her.

She passes by me—
I smell her fragrance.
Again she gives me a quick glance and a smile.
My heart heaves faster;
Droplets of sweat bead my forehead.

She struts toward the door and disappears—

Her fragrance and smile linger behind, statue-like.

YOU

You are here,
There,
And everywhere.

Without you
I am bare,
Nowhere
And without a clue.

HOMELESS

Against the tarnished
White wall, Luanne leaned;
She saw the sky lunge
Burnished lances at her,
Turning her skin into
Crocodile hide,
Unshaven upper lip into
Water-dripping grass.

Against the tarnished
White wall, Luanne leaned;
She stared at the tails
Of nonchalance from
Burrowed eyes.

Seeing no recourse
To reverse the tide
Of misfortune, she
Breathed a little,
Sighed a little,
Listened to the swallows
A little.

Against the tarnished
White wall, Luanne leaned;
Against Time, she swam.

THE UNKNOWN MATE

Face unglossed,
Her skin glows as raw milk,
Her eyes are pristine
As mountain lakes.

She worships the blooms
Of daisies,
Shuns the glitter of doubloons.

She is more inebriated by the
Scent of pine trees than
Blended perfumes.

She prefers wearing stitched
Canvas to embroidered cashmere.

She has the bottomless patience
Of saints,
The unbroken care of nuns.

Tempted,
She retires into the bower of loyalty.

CONSEQUENCES

I keep storing
Things
In the recesses
Of my closets;
They turn dusty,
Moth-afflicted,
Waiting—

Like unspent emotions.

MUTUAL ATTRACTION

What do you see in him?

The eloquence of his gold,
The elegance of his platinum,
The romance of his diamonds,
The touch of his silk.

What do you see in her?

The gold of her eloquence,
The platinum of her elegance,
The diamonds of her romance,
The silk of her touch.

BRASSIERE

Two pouches strung as one;
It is home for the comfort-
Conscious; it delineates the
Role it plays in our civilization:
Subtle bounces were once
Permitted—
Within its confines.

Gravitational pull
Takes its toll
As the years
Empty what was full.

MADAM!

A beautician can do
Only so much for you;
It's no use to blame
The lag in
Cosmetic technology.

MODERN GODS

Every week
She buys for herself
A new body and
A new mind from:

The nutrition expert,
      The masseuse,
The aerobic dance instructor,
      And the psychiatrist.

AT THE PARK

At the well-kept park,
They sit on a wooden bench;
Their shrunken heads rest
On desiccated torsos, bony
Hands clutching mahogany
Canes; a paisley shawl
Wraps around her shoulders,
A vaudevillian hat perches
Uneasily on his tonsured scalp.

Oblivious to the baby squirrel
Frolicking nearby, their dimming
Eyes roam memories of a life gone by.

TO MY BELOVED

I spent my youthful years
Negotiating the jungles
Of your mind.

I spent my adult years
Running on the highways
Of your mind.

I spent my mellow years
Strolling on the prairies
Of your mind.

Now I am spending my twilight years
Crawling on the desert
Of your mind;

Let me know where you are,
Let me know before the twilight turns to night.

MONDAY

She is gone—
Again.
I stare at her image.
Friday night—
A millennium away!

A GREY GATHERING

We sat in ancient couches,
Scintillating witticisms,
Spelling out poetic kens,
Whipping worries to martyrdom.

At the dining table,
Where cuisine vied for attention
With verses,
Grey leaped out of thinning crowns,

And women, ah women,
Ribbons of steam,
Spiraling from teacups.

LURE ME NOT

Lure me not, ebony Moon, lure me not,
Into the dungeon of love. I've served my time;
My tears have grooved my pillow.
The years have sieved my heart.
The steel bars have blinded my eyesight
And blunted my senses.

I've shaken off the harness,
Shed my striped uniform, and
Worn the white silk of freedom.

Lead me not
To the wise men of the mind;
Let their gilded gibberish
Fall on waxed ears.

I shall sink my fingers
Into the soil
And uproot the rosebud of seduction.

APPEARANCES

The Rolex watch he wore
Was always visible and
Heavy gold chains swung constantly
On his grey-haired chest.
He wore a bright silk shirt
And an Armani suit;
A hybrid perpetual rose
Was always on his lapel.

He drove a bright latest-model Porsche,
And whenever he stepped out of his car,
He made sure a copy of "Town and Country"
Was on his front seat.

When he walked down the street
He always carried a copy of the
"Wall Street Journal."

His girlfriend, a beautiful young blonde,
Always accompanied his trips and strolls.

But, when she grew tired of unfulfilled love
And carried on with a young man,
He broke down and cried.

SHE CRIED, I CRIED

When I was twenty-four springs,
I thought love belonged
In books and in the movies,
And when she said:
"I love you; you know that!"
I laughed and said: "What?"
She cried and cried.

When I was four winters
Shy from forty
And she moved away,
I cried and cried.

MARITAL POSTURES

They sleep
> With their bodies interlocked.

They sleep
> With their bodies separated.

The sleep
> Back to back.

They sleep
> In separate beds.

They sleep
> In different rooms.

They sleep
> In different buildings.

JUST MARRIED

Solemnly at the altar they glow.
Solemnly to the lawyers they go.

SO SOON

Are you leaving?
 So soon!
Your eyes say
So soon!
Let our forms
Commune
Before they
Burn and fume.

TRAPPED

This is how
My mind works:
Open yours and
Accept it or
Leave it alone;
Cruel is the
Game we play,
Forlorn is the
Name of the bed
We sleep in

You may slam the
Door behind you.
Or break the flower
Vase; our frayed
Nerves will soon
Boil over, and
When the lid blows
Off, the pieces
Will scatter far
And wide.

Tears and regrets
Are too weak
To clear our way.

THE END

We nourished the illusion
That we were inseparable
Until we were consumed by it.

Soon we will go separately,
But I will think of you
As long as my blood flows.

Our lives will be laden
With uncertainties; we may
Each in our own way still
Blame each other for our
Difficulties. There will
Be only notoriously unresponsive
Shadows to attack.

We will write our life stories
Silently on the disjointed bones
Of our dreams.

LEAVING ME

In the hollow of the night,
I chisel your face—
Radiant as the sun.
I look you straight in the eye
And I say: Why?

I sculpt your hands
And hold them
And I say: Why?

You stare at me.
Your hands shake and sweat,
And you whisper: "Had I known . . . ."
There is pause, silence.
You dissolve slowly—
And fade away like a ghost.

I place my head on my pillow;
My eyes close tight
And my wet palms, clenched,
Rest on my bed.

PARTING

Love!
Before I leave,
Let me look at
Your face.

Your image
Will klieg-light
My journey in the
Dark alleyways
Ahead.

RISKY BUSINESS

An affair is
Temporary welfare;
Seldom faring well
Often leading to
Curses and wails,
Segue to playing
Solitaire.

THE LAST MANGO IN PARIS

At the Champs Elysees café,
Once I settled in the chair,
My eyes caught the aura
Of pedigree, the insouciance,
The indolence.

Haute couture,
Blue-lace white chapeau
Tilting to the right
Shadowing diamond-studded
Earrings,
Dark glasses resting
On sun-kissed cheeks;
A soupçon of tan clinging
To her alabaster neck;
Slim, ringed fingers
Hold a shiny knife,
Sculpturing a mango
Into long strips,
Peeling the skin,
Forking the yellow flesh
And placing it
Between her pink lips,
Chewing it slowly,
Ever so slowly.

Garçon! Garçon!
A mango like that, s'il vous plait!

AROUND THE WORLD AND BACK

From the Swiss Alps
To the Blue Danube
I hover,
On the Yangtze
I row,
On the Nile
I glide.

I ogle strawberry and platinum blondes,
Befriend browns and reds, and hues in between
As they float on streams of splendor, and
Strut on cushions of luxury.
I sample the delicacies, and do not pray for more.

Cloudy and cerulean skies ferry me back.

Across my window,
In the Goleta Valley,
Where brown grass meets concrete
And swallows trill on power lines,
I see her stroll into my soul.
With palpitating heart, I run and run;
I stretch my hands, she nods and smiles.

ZSA ZSA

Her platinum crown
May obscure strands of silver,
But high cheekbones
Mock time's attrition.

Her waxed, sophisticated beauty
Exudes an aura of rustic simplicity.

Her accented speech often
Draws attention and smiles.

When she lures diamonds
To her golden bower
She is unaware that fortune
Speaks two tongues.

When she drives her pink Rolls Royce
She pays no homage to the world beyond;
She courts the sting of law
With a child's insouciance
And sojourns in a chamber
Where armed guards
Bow neither to glamour nor wealth.

ELIZABETH TAYLOR

Men swooned
Under her mascaraed gaze
And in her scented garden,
They dreamt the night
Would not end.

She discarded them
And they mused.

Marriage was a fairy
That resided in the
Bowels of a desert
Mirage.

She retreated
Into Cleopatra's chamber
And the world fantasized;
She argued in
Virginia's living-room
And it marveled at her
Tongue and mettle.

Time may have
Graveled her alabaster skin,
Silvered her ebony hair,
And puffed her smooth cheeks,

But her violets
Shall never dim nor wilt.

JACQUELINE KENNEDY

A queen in a land
Where palaces are
Relegated to the
Slipstream of history;

An apotheosis in the
Pantheon of first ladies,
Egregiously feminine,
Unambiguously elegant,
Evoking images of glamour
And power.

Standing her ground,
Weathering the emotional
Maelstrom, when the assassin's
Bullet found its mark and
The president succumbed.

The shrapnel remains
Lodged in our consciousness.

MARILYN MONROE

We genuflected
Before
Her pulchritude.

We sacrificed her
When she began to mirror
Our own weaknesses.

Her death enabled us
To resume our devotion
To the myth.

CHASING WOMEN

Yesterday
I chased women
With my body.

Today
I chase them
With my eyes.

Tomorrow
I will chase them
With my memory.

OVER FIFTY

When you are over fifty
You learn to deploy
Your remaining resources more wisely
For the rougher road ahead—
That peace and serenity
You have read and heard about
All your life.

You consult your mind less and less
In favor of your back and legs;
You remember fondly the days
When you could climb the stairs
Without hearing a squeak
Or gasping for a breath.

You learn not to cross borders
Without a thorough scrutiny
Of what lies miles and miles beyond.

The absences in your life
Remind you of vulnerabilities;
And you learn to step on the ground gingerly.

PASSAGE

The veins under her skin
Are bone-dry tributaries
Of a river long plagued by drought.

Her eyes are lagoons
Encircled by the advancing pleats
On her cheeks and forehead.

Her breasts resemble gloves
Whose erstwhile inhabitants
Have moved on to a life
Of retired stardom.

Her once blond crown
Is now a snow-covered cedar.

Tiny red moons embellish
The backs of her hands.

She walks straight and steady;
She speaks with
A forceful and measured tone.

SENIOR

Old,
Not dead,
Not yet anyway,
But even if she were,
One may see the beauty
On her cheeks—those lines,
Concentric lines as if
They were wrought by a spider;
And grooves around her mouth,
The sediments of Time
Ensconcing the words
She once spoke,
The silences she kept
As she went through
The breezes and the blizzards.

DECORATIVE FIGURE ON AN ORNAMENTAL BACKGROUND

A PAINTING BY HENRI MATISSE

A Cultural Fascination or a Plea For Female
Manumission

The odalisque adds to the floral rug; she is the
Object of curiosity that degenerates into
A concupiscent fantasy.

The virtuoso exposes
An abusive culture where women are
Coercively relegated to satisfying the
Male's needs; she trumpets:

Oh, World!
Oh, Humanity!
Come, come,
Come to me
And deliver me
From this savagery.

LOOKING BACK

I have walked the plains
And climbed the hills,
I have separated the gold
From the dross,
I have lived in dreams
And survived the deserts,
I have cried aloud
And written poetry,
I have praised love
And denounced its vagaries—

Yet, should I expire
Before re-inhaling its aroma,
Touching its petals in my grave
Would for me suffice.

AFTER YOU'RE GONE

I
Rummage
Through
My
Inner
Files.
I
Discover
You
Occupy
Every
Page.

ANGEL

My angel arrived;
I saw the wings flutter,
I felt the air,
Drizzles of air
Bouncing about my face.
My eyelashes quivered.
As I palmed my face,
Swirls of breeze passed
Through my fingers
Like strings of pearls.
Sluices of light
Hovered over my head,
My angel,
Messenger of the Purple Skies,
Keeper of the Jeweled Gate.

A SPLASH OF JASMINE

Life, ah, life!

A splash of jasmine;

It evaporates

            Before

We are able to inhale

All of its power.

ACKNOWLEDGMENT

Judy, the indispensable partner

    YOU

    You are here,
    There,
    And everywhere.

    Without you
    I am bare,
    Nowhere
    And without a clue.

BIOGRAPHY

Mahdy Y. Khaiyat holds degrees from the University of California, Santa Barbara, and is a freelance editor and translator.

He started writing poetry in 1990. The publication of his first poem in a literary magazine in the same year encouraged him to continue writing. His poems have since been published in periodicals in the United States, Canada, Australia, France, Japan, Belgium, England, Finland, New Zealand, and Argentina.